7 STARTER STEPS

On Your Journey To A NEW YOU

Breaking The Average Life MENTORS

Written by Kristy Griffiths BTALM Team 2024

Email: btal.journey@gmail.com

Prologue

Imagine waking up each day with a sense of purpose, knowing you're creating a life you're proud of, a life that feels true to who you are. Most of us spend years searching for that feeling, chasing after it in our careers, relationships, and even our daily routines. Yet, more often than not, we end up feeling disconnected from the person we aspire to be. This book is about bridging that gap, about peeling back the layers that have accumulated over time—the doubts, the fears, the beliefs that have held us back. It's about uncovering the version of ourselves we've always dreamed of but weren't sure how to reach.

The journey won't be perfect, nor will it be easy. Change requires honesty, resilience, and most importantly, a willingness to keep moving forward even when the path is unclear. This is not about overnight success or quick fixes. It's about cultivating a new mindset, adopting habits that empower rather than hinder, and taking small, consistent steps toward a better version of yourself. Each step builds on the last, creating a powerful foundation for lasting transformation.

7 Starter Steps On Your Journey To You

These "7 Starter Habits" aren't just a to-do list; they're a framework for embracing your potential. They guide you to ask the right questions, shake up old routines, and take action with courage and intention. Whether you're at the beginning of your personal growth journey or somewhere along the way, these habits are here to support, uplift, and challenge you to be your best self.

So, are you ready? The journey to you begins now.

Written by: Kristy Griffiths

7 Starter Steps On your journey to a new you:

"Unlocking Your Potential: 7 Habits to Transform Your Life and Discover the Real You!"

Table Of Contents

Introduction

In this ever-moving, ever-shaking world, there often comes a moment when we pause and ask ourselves if the race is worth the cost. We find ourselves busy, our schedules filled to the brim, yet when we look at our lives, true satisfaction feels elusive. Life is buzzing around us, but inwardly we feel as though we're moving in slow motion. And then, the question inevitably comes up... *Why?*

Why work so hard? Why keep going? Why fight for every step? When each move seems to bring us no closer to joy and fulfilment and only adds to our stress, it feels as if we're trapped in a cycle that has no end. Even when we try to take a breather, something new demands our energy, our focus, our "all."

If you've reached this point in your life—the point where you're ready for a change—then know that this is your time to reclaim your path, your priorities, and your peace. Real transformation doesn't happen overnight, but it begins with small steps that guide us back to ourselves, back to purpose, and back to genuine fulfilment. This is your invitation to begin that journey.

Here are 7 simple ways to start your journey to *you* and finally experience the true richness of life. These habits are designed to help you realign with what truly matters, making the road back to yourself clear, intentional, and inspiring.

Step 1

Connect to Your Source

For me, this journey began in 2017, just before the world was rocked by the COVID-19 pandemic. I had just given birth to my fifth child, Michael, and although family life filled me with joy, I knew I was still missing something. I felt fulfilled as a mother but unfulfilled financially and personally. Deep down, I knew a change was needed.

Life moved on around me at its usual, relentless pace. Days were a whirlwind of demands, noise, and responsibilities, and finding even a moment's peace seemed impossible with five kids, a husband, and a business. I kept wondering where I could go to reflect, to think, to reconnect with myself. How would I even begin?

That's when my grandmother's house came to mind. Nestled miles away from the city, her home had always been a place of peace and simplicity. It was quiet, isolated, and far removed from the hustle and bustle that had consumed me. And I always felt a deep connection there to the land, to my ancestors, to the parts of myself I often ignored.

So, every weekend, I started making the trip. The house had been abandoned for some time, but I decided to fix it up, bit by bit. As I repaired the walls and painted the rooms, I felt as though I was mending my own spirit, piece by piece. It became a project of both revival and self-discovery. Working on that old house helped me see that I was rebuilding myself.

The quietness there was profound—no electricity, no devices buzzing, just stillness. In that peaceful silence, I found the space to think without the usual clutter clouding my mind. The noise of the world faded, allowing me to reconnect with the deepest parts of myself.

Finding Your Own Source

Connecting to your source is all about finding a sanctuary that allows you to pause, breathe, and reflect. This place can be anywhere that brings you peace: a room in your house, a corner in your garden, or even a quiet space in your mind that you access through meditation. What matters is that it is a place where you can truly disconnect from the world, letting go of all its demands and distractions.

Creating this space, wherever it may be, will help you tune out the background noise and listen to your own thoughts. You'll begin to see things clearly, understand what you truly want, and recognize the changes you need to make. This is where you'll begin to make decisions that align with your deepest desires, guiding your life onto a path that fulfils not only your own needs but those of your family and your dreams.

Step 2

Dream It... Believe It... Speak It

Now that you've connected with your source, you've glimpsed something powerful—there is more to life than you once imagined. This is where dreaming comes in, where your vision of the life you want begins to unfold. Albert Einstein once said, *"Imagination is a preview of life's coming attractions,"* and it's true—our dreams are the seeds of what we can make real.

Allow yourself to dream deeply. Picture the life you want: the places you want to see, the experiences you crave, the home you imagine building, the people you envision beside you. Visualize the small details: the scent of the ocean air on that beach you hope to visit, the warm glow of a room that feels like home, the flavors of meals shared with loved ones, and the laughter that echoes around you. Let yourself feel the sensations of this life, engaging all your senses to bring it to life in your mind.

This kind of dreaming isn't just for enjoyment; it's a crucial step. We are emotional beings, and we are driven by our senses. Remarkably, the mind can't easily distinguish between what we vividly imagine and what we actually experience. When you dream with this level of detail, you're giving your mind a taste of what could be, and that taste is incredibly motivating.

From Dreaming to Believing

For many of us, it's easy to stop at the dreaming stage. It's thrilling to imagine a different life, to spend time "living it up" in our minds. But the next, crucial step is to believe that these dreams are possible for you. Often, this is where we stumble. Our past experiences, the limitations we've grown up with, and the negative self-talk we've absorbed can hold us back. But here's the truth: you are worthy of the life you imagine. You are made with the same capacity to create, achieve, and thrive as anyone else. If others can build lives they love, you can too.

My question to you is: **Why not you?** If you can dream it, then you are already capable of pursuing it. Faith in yourself and your vision is essential here. Past experiences and setbacks don't determine your future. With the right mindset, you can break through old patterns, rise above limitations, and create the life you truly desire.

Think back on times when you wanted something deeply and committed to achieving it. Maybe it wasn't perfect, maybe it wasn't even right for you, but if you pursued it with determination, you probably found a way to make it yours. That same strength is in you now, waiting for you to channel it toward something that genuinely fulfils you.

Speaking It into Existence

As you begin to believe, take it a step further and start speaking your dreams out loud. Declare what you want confidently, as if it's already on its way. Speaking it aloud gives your dreams power and makes them feel tangible. Say to yourself, *"I am on my way to the life I envision. I am capable, deserving, and ready."*

Use your dreams to fuel your journey forward, even when things are tough. By actively dreaming, believing, and speaking your aspirations, you'll find strength to push through the present, no matter how challenging it may be. Remember, this is your journey, and every small step you take to make your dream a reality brings you closer to the life you're truly meant to live.

Step 3

Take Stock of Your Life

"Eliminate the Unnecessary"

At this stage in your journey, it's time to pause, reflect, and take an honest inventory of your life. Look closely at where you are right now—no excuses, no filters, just pure acceptance. You may not be where you hoped or planned to be, but this is your reality, and acknowledging it without blame or shame is crucial. Remember, *"Acceptance is the first step to improvement."*

For years before I truly committed to change, I had this nagging feeling that something wasn't right. I sensed that I was doing things wrong, that certain habits and decisions were holding me back, yet I wasn't ready to face the truth. Instead, I brushed off my own role in the matter, and instead I placed the blame elsewhere—on the government, my upbringing, my circumstances, even my age. I blamed anything that allowed me to avoid looking inward. But as time went on, things only got worse, and I knew deep down that real change could only start from within.

One night, as I scrolled through YouTube, I stumbled upon a talk by Joseph P. Washington, where he defined "average" as *"the top of the bottom and the bottom of the top."* His words hit me hard. I realized that I was living right there—in the comfort of mediocrity. It was the wake-up call I needed. I decided to stop blaming everything and everyone else and take responsibility. Because if the problem was me, then I could change me. I couldn't change the world around me, but I could change my own habits and approach, one small step at a time.

Taking Stock: Evaluating Your Habits

Taking stock means taking a close, honest look at your habits and actions—both the ones that serve you and the ones that hold you back. Recognize that change requires shedding the habits that no longer serve your growth. This is an intentional process: think of it as a "life detox," keeping only what strengthens and supports your journey forward.

We all know, deep down, the habits that no longer serve us. It's time to identify them and start letting go. Here are some common habits that might be holding you back:

Negative Habits to Eliminate:

- Questionable or unsupportive friendships

- Overindulgence in drinking or smoking

- Hours spent on social media

- Excessive TV or gaming

- Gossiping

- Pretending to work without purpose

- Worrying about things out of your control

- Procrastination

- Self-doubt

Eliminating these habits is a significant step toward becoming your best self. Cutting out what drains your energy and brings you down clears space for new, empowering behaviours to take root.

Some Positive Habits to Keep:

- Willingness to work hard

- Desire for personal growth

- Dreaming big and envisioning the life you want

- Believing in yourself and your ability to change

Continuously Check In with Yourself

Moving forward means consistently asking yourself a powerful question: *"Is what I'm doing right now moving me toward or away from the life I want?"* It's a reminder to keep yourself on track, to stay mindful of how each action impacts your goals. As motivational speaker Jim Rohn wisely said, *"Don't blame the seed, don't blame the soil, don't blame the water—because it's all you have."* Instead, focus on using what you have to create the life you desire.

Crafting a Plan with "New Eyes"

Taking stock gives you the clarity and insight you need to design a new plan, one that aligns with your goals and values. With fresh eyes and a new mindset, you can approach change one manageable step at a time. Imagine each change as laying a brick, just like the builders of grand cathedrals who laid each stone, one by one. Great things are built gradually, over time.

Never underestimate the power of "one by one." Start today. Make a small change, then build upon it tomorrow. Before you know it, these small steps will accumulate into a life that looks and feels closer to your dreams.

Step 4

Shake the Ground You Walk On

As humans, we're wired to seek comfort. Our instincts drive us toward routines, predictability, and safety, sparing ourselves from the unsettling feeling of uncertainty. Most of us know this all too well—the steady job, the familiar lunch spot, the same conversations. We stick to what we know, retreating from anything that challenges that comfort zone.

But here's the thing: on your journey to becoming your true self, breaking out of these patterns is essential. Growth requires us to step off the well-worn path and into the unknown, to deliberately "shake the ground we walk on." Life is an adventure, a journey! By embracing this, we invite excitement, discovery, and transformation.

Now, I know it sounds daunting. Comfort zones are deeply ingrained, and changing routines feels like facing a wall. But the beauty of being human is our ability to change in ways no other species can. Unlike animals, whose instincts govern every action, we can decide in a single moment to pivot, to forge a new path. A bird can't change its song; a dog can't stop barking. But you? You can change everything about your direction, purpose, and perspective in an instant.

You can be driving to work and decide, "Nope, I'm heading to the beach instead." That level of freedom is uniquely ours. *Shaking the ground you walk on* means doing something different, however small, to break the habitual patterns that hold you back and spark a shift in your thinking.

Start Small to Rewire Your Mind

Sudden, dramatic changes can shock the system, which can make the mind push back. Instead, try easing into change through small, simple shifts. Experiment with little disruptions to your routine: have a different lunch, take a cold shower, or drive a different route to work. These small shifts gently rewire your mind to see that change doesn't have to be threatening—it can be thrilling.

The mind is constantly working to keep us "safe," so tricking it into accepting new habits is best done gradually. Even something as minor as taking a new path to work can create a ripple effect. You see different surroundings, notice things you wouldn't otherwise, and open yourself to the chance of new opportunities. Who knows? That unexpected turn might lead to a chance meeting with someone who could change your life.

When you make small changes, it's like flipping a switch in your brain. Your senses sharpen, and life feels more vibrant. And as you take these steps, you'll feel a growing sense of control, fuelling your journey with excitement and momentum.

Breaking Free from the Ordinary

When I was ready for a bigger change, I decided to move out of the neighbourhood I'd lived in for years. I needed a fresh start, new perspectives, and an environment that fuelled my personal growth. For you, change doesn't have to be that big, but it does need to be meaningful. Challenge yourself to try something that disrupts your ordinary rhythm. Try a new sport, read a different type of book, or surprise your kids by stopping at a park on the way home.

As you shake things up, remember the saying, *"If you keep doing the same things, you'll keep getting the same results."* Change requires action, and action starts with a single step outside your comfort zone.

The Power of Small Adventures

Each time you step into something new, your brain gets a fresh input—a different flavour, a new sight, a new feeling. These small adventures build up, sparking curiosity and widening your world. You'll start seeing the endless possibilities around you. That tiny shift in perspective may set off a cascade of positive changes, pushing you further along your journey with renewed energy and purpose.

Try It Today

Reading this isn't enough. So, I encourage you to take a small action today that feels new or a bit daring. Even the simplest shift can ignite the spirit of adventure within you and start changing your outlook on life. Life is an adventure, so embrace it! Do something different, think differently, dare to be different, and watch how your world opens up.

Step 5

Follow Your Passion

From as far back as I can remember, I loved anything that involved trading, buying, and selling. Business was my game—even as a kid. My cousins and I would play Monopoly for hours during summer, and when we weren't playing board games, we'd turn the house into a pretend grocery store. On the other hand, video games like Mortal Kombat? Let's just say I was terrible at them, and I didn't care to get better because they didn't light me up the same way. Those childhood summers revealed something important about myself: I wasn't interested in working for anyone. I was driven by the idea of creating my own path.

So I got started early, selling juice outside my house like the classic lemonade stand you see on TV. That first little venture was enough to show me that my passion was real and I could go far if I stuck with it. Eventually, I moved on to open a small snack stand, and after that, I dreamed of opening my own grocery store. Other business opportunities came along, and I jumped in headfirst, loving every moment because I was pursuing something I truly enjoyed. Up until COVID-19 hit, I thought I was set. But when the pandemic threw my financial stability into question, I realized I couldn't rely on chance to protect my freedom. I knew I needed to build something strong enough to withstand life's uncertainties.

So, I took a hard look at myself, my habits, and my knowledge gaps. I accepted that if I wanted to reach the next level, I needed more than passion—I needed knowledge, wisdom, and a commitment to continual growth. I turned to self-help and motivational resources, reading books and listening to speakers who had faced similar challenges and achieved the success I envisioned for myself. These resources became my teachers, helping me to level up faster by learning from others' experiences. Now, I've made a lifelong commitment to learning. There's a unique magic in studying other people's journeys; it shows you that the path is there, waiting for you.

"Follow Your Passion" is More than a Cliché

Growing up, I constantly heard the advice to "follow your dreams" or "listen to your heart," but I believe the true key to a fulfilling life is following your *passion*. Passion is different because it's not just about the things you want or like; it's about the things that feel natural to you, almost effortless. It's that one thing that you'd do every day, without tiring, simply because it brings you joy.

For some, it could be cooking up delicious meals, making people laugh, fixing things, listening to others' stories, or organizing events. What's beautiful about passion is that it's unique for everyone, like a personal compass guiding you to a meaningful path. In today's world, many of these seemingly "small" passions have become thriving careers. Why? Because people have discovered that following what they're truly good at opens doors they didn't even know existed.

When I think back on my life, I see that business was my first passion, but as I grew older, I discovered another just as powerful—helping people feel inspired. I didn't realize at first that I had a knack for encouraging others to love God and find strength in themselves through life's challenges. I started out encouraging friends, but I soon found myself talking to the mirror, giving myself pep talks, almost as if I were speaking to someone else. One day, I finally felt brave enough to record a video and post it on YouTube and TikTok. I still remember walking into my office and telling my sister, "People, I am in the world now!" It felt empowering, even though that first video didn't go viral.

The response didn't matter to me as much as the feeling of authenticity. Posting that video was a small step, but it was a big moment in realizing my passion. As Steve Harvey says, "Your gift will make room for you," and I knew this was my gift. I didn't need a million views to see that this was my path—it was enough that it felt right, like I was finally aligning with my purpose.

Identify Your Passion and Turn It Into Your Path

How do you find your passion? Start by listing the activities that bring you joy. Think about those things that come naturally, that spark energy within you. Look for the tasks that don't feel like work but rather play, even when they require effort. Your passion doesn't have to be something big or complex; it can be as simple as cooking, storytelling, being good with numbers, or having an eye for design. Notice how many of these interests have become real-world careers. There's a reason for that: people have realized that they can bring their unique gifts to the world and thrive doing what they love.

Here's what we recommend:

1. **Make a List**: Write down everything you enjoy doing, even if it seems small or insignificant. This can include things you've always loved since childhood or hobbies you've picked up over the years.

 2. **Choose the One that Feels Effortless**: Look over your list and find the activity that you could do all day without feeling drained. That's the one that aligns most closely with your passion.

3. **Practice and Develop It**: Pursue this passion with intention. Start taking small steps to build on it, whether that means practicing more, learning from others, or sharing it with the world in small ways.

4. Become Your Passion: Don't be afraid to fully step into it. Whether it's through creating content, offering a service, or just sharing your gift with friends and family, let your passion become a bigger part of who you are.

Trust That Your Passion Will Lead the Way

Our world is full of possibilities, and there's a place for every unique passion. When you follow yours, it won't just feel fulfilling; it will open up opportunities and bring abundance into your life. You'll be amazed at the doors that begin to open, often when you least expect them. Trust your passion to guide you; it's your own special path toward creating the life you desire.

Take Action Today

Today, decide to follow your passion. Try something that feels like an expression of who you are. Let yourself be pulled by that energy, knowing that every little step adds up to create a life that's not just successful but also deeply satisfying. Remember, the world needs your unique gifts—

embrace them, develop them, and watch your life transform.

Step 6

Take Action

Once I accepted that change was necessary, something shifted inside me. Suddenly, I was asking myself questions I'd never considered before: "I know I need to change if I want my life to improve, but where do I even begin? How do I start?" These questions were the seeds of something powerful because they opened my mind to new possibilities. I realized that when we ask questions with genuine intent, our minds begin to look for answers. It's like setting off a chain reaction that draws solutions toward us, one step at a time.

At first, I began noticing things I'd previously overlooked—ads for books, motivational talks, local events, even small bookstores I'd never paid attention to before. This isn't magic; it's how the mind works. When you give it a new problem, it starts searching for ways to solve it, bringing new ideas and insights into focus. I started tuning in to motivational speakers on YouTube, like Jim Rohn and Jordan B. Peterson, and picked up a few pocket-sized daily readers on life and spirituality. They were small actions, but each one added fuel to my momentum.

Starting Small—Setting the Wheels in Motion

I still remember the first time I decided to act on my desire for change. I set my alarm for 5:00 AM, unsure what I would do but determined to start. When the alarm went off, I told myself, "This is the beginning of the rest of your life, Kristy. Give it a shot." I got out of bed, opened one of those books, and read a few pages. Then, I spent a few minutes in prayer, asking for guidance and expressing gratitude for the journey ahead. It was a small routine, but it felt incredibly grounding.

By the time my husband and kids started waking up around 6:00 AM, I had already given myself an hour of peace and positivity. I felt calmer, more focused, and even a little excited. Those quiet moments gave me a sense of ownership over my day and my life. Soon, I was getting up before my alarm, eager to have that precious time to myself. After about ten days, I wanted more—I increased my quiet time to 4:00 AM, then 3:00 AM. Now, I'm not suggesting that everyone needs to wake up at that hour, but for me, the quiet hours are precious. Living in the country and managing school schedules means I need to start my day early, and this routine has become the foundation of my new life.

Transforming Thought into Action

What I discovered is that once you're truly ready to change, the right actions reveal themselves. In those early hours, I began planning my day, setting goals, and writing down everything that came to mind, from tasks like calling the bank or buying office supplies to brainstorming ideas for my business. The list sometimes included people's names, little nudges from the universe telling me who I should reach out to or follow up with. Listening to these nudges created a domino effect—every small action pushed me further forward, each step connecting to the next.

Consistency Builds Momentum

As the days turned into weeks, these small, consistent actions created powerful momentum. Each morning, I continued my routine: praying, reading, writing, and listening to motivational talks. I didn't just focus on tasks but on building a mindset for growth and perseverance. Over time, I saw how even minor changes in my habits rippled through my life, bringing new opportunities and insights I hadn't anticipated.

When I plan my day in the quiet morning hours, I jot down everything that comes to mind, even if it seems trivial. Here are a few examples:

- Call the bank to discuss finances

- Schedule professional headshots

- Restock office supplies

- Draft a business proposal

- Update my business's social media page

- Follow up with clients about pending payments

- Reach out to an old friend who popped into my mind

If I can't accomplish everything on my list that day, I roll it over to the next. The key isn't to do everything perfectly; it's about building momentum. With each step, I'm nurturing a cycle of positivity and productivity, gaining more confidence in my direction.

Listen to Your Inner Guidance

Your journey will look different from mine, but the principle remains the same: trust your intuition. Those small inner promptings are guiding you toward the steps unique to your own path. Start by asking yourself the questions that matter: What do you truly want? Where do you see yourself going? What's the first small step you can take to move forward?

When you listen to your intuition, you give yourself permission to discover answers that may surprise you. Don't expect overnight transformations; instead, embrace the journey. By taking action, you're laying the groundwork for something larger than each small step—a life aligned with your values, dreams, and inner purpose.

So today, take a moment, set your alarm, or do something different that aligns with the change you want. Remember, your mind is incredibly powerful. Give it a clear direction, take those first small steps, and watch as your actions propel you forward on the path to your best life.

Step 7:

Keep It Moving

"Don't Stop, Don't Quit"

On the journey to becoming your best self, there will inevitably be times—many times—when you doubt yourself. You might wonder, "Am I doing the right things? Is this even working? Am I getting anywhere?" These questions are normal, and if you're on this path alone, they can feel even heavier. The truth is, every worthwhile journey comes with moments of self-doubt. My mentor, Jim Rohn, always says: "Trust the process." It took years to get to the point where you realized change was necessary, and it won't happen overnight. Your current situation is the result of countless choices—some unwise or unintentional. Now, creating the life you want will take a series of conscious, intentional decisions. You're in this for the long haul, and each small, consistent action adds up.

As you grow, you may notice that doubts don't just come from within. There will be people around you—your own "Doubters Fan Club." Some will silently hope you fail, and others might even tell you that your goals are a waste of time. Their words can hit hard, but don't let them sink in. The journey to personal growth often shines a spotlight on other people's insecurities, too. When they see you rising, it may remind them of their own stagnation or past failures. Stand firm in your decisions, and don't let the voices of others steer you off your path. You have something special in you that's worth protecting.

And let's not forget about the "moods" that creep up along the way. There will be days when you're not just doubting your journey but also feeling overwhelmed by negative emotions. You might ask yourself, "Is this worth it? Why even try if every day feels like a battle?" This is normal, too. As Jordan B. Peterson puts it, "It's your best bet! Do you have anything better to do than aim for the greatest good?" The road can feel rough and relentless at times, and yes, things can always get worse if you don't address them. But remember, by working on yourself, you're choosing the path that can also make things 100 times better. Sure, it takes effort and consistency, but it's worth every ounce of energy if it brings you closer to peace, fulfilment, and purpose.

When things feel like they're at a standstill or even moving backward, remind yourself of how far you've come. Trusting the process means recognizing that growth isn't a straight line; there will be ups, downs, and even detours along the way. But every step forward, no matter how small, is still progress. Sometimes, progress looks like a zigzag. Sometimes it's two steps forward and one step back. But even with those setbacks, you're still further along than you were yesterday. And that's worth celebrating.

The best way to keep moving forward is to do just that—keep moving. If you have a rough day, pick yourself up and move on. As Peterson also says, "Start stopping right now"—stop believing the doubters, stop feeding the negative thoughts, and start putting one foot in front of the other again. When you hit a rough patch, take a deep breath, reassess, and keep going. Just one small step forward—anything that keeps the momentum alive.

The road to your dreams doesn't have a finish line because self-improvement is a lifelong journey. Some days will test your patience, and others will fill you with pride and excitement. The path may twist and turn, but as long as you're moving, you're growing. Look at today and see how far you've come, even if you've faced some setbacks. You're still moving up.

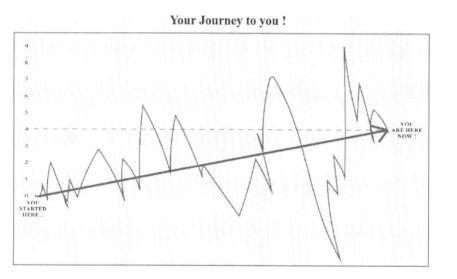

Your Journey to you !

So, keep it moving. Don't stop. Don't quit.

Make today another step in your journey toward the life you want and the person you're meant to become.

The best days are ahead of you...

if you just keep going...

7
STARTER
STEPS

On Your Journey To A NEW YOU

Made in the USA
Columbia, SC
13 January 2025